NOTES FROM THE
CAT HOUSE

My thanks to Carolyn Hinsey and Estha Weiner for their guidance.
And to the late Bob Booth, for suggesting this in the first place.

Macabre Ink is an imprint of Crossroad Press.

Copyright © 2014 by Jack Ketchum
Cover by David Dodd
Design by Aaron Rosenberg
ISBN 978-1-941408-09-4 — ISBN 978-1-941408-10-0 (pbk.)
For information address Crossroad Press at 141 Brayden Dr., Hertford, NC 27944
www.crossroadpress.com

First edition

NOTES FROM THE
CAT HOUSE

POEMS
BY
JACK KETCHUM

Author's Note

Some of these poems have been previously published, in altered form, in *The Devil's Wine*, edited by Tom Piccirilli, *Hint Fiction*, edited by Robert Swartwood, on the Spiderwords website, edited by Rain Graves, and in chapbook form by Gauntlet Books, Barry Hoffman, editor.

Table of Contents

Introduction

Johnnie Mack Brown

Hoboe's Memoir

When I Am A Boy

Arthur

KU

KU Two

11/11/87

Announcement

Beast

Contact

Cats Hide Nothing

Sleeping Woman

Fireflies

Hearts

For Caity

Christmas Day, 1969

To Lance And Cathy's Child On The Afternoon Of Her Birth, July 9th, 1970

Billy's Dad

Bethel, New York, August 16, 1969

A Terrible Thing

Wings

Michou

An Honest Word

Dreams The Luna Moth

Mondo Cane

St. John

Greece

Sword And Sandal

Cats' Haiku For Paula On The Road

Question

Second Virgin

Rehearsal, Marat/Sade, 1969

Poetic

TV Guide

Mathematics

Vinni

Tragedy

The Teacher, 1969

Crisis

For Cujo

M.D.

Walk

Bethel, New York , August 16, 1969

Janis

A Promise

Morning Star

Imperatives

On "The Gates," NYC

Catskill Morning Observation

The Letter

Clocking

Imperatives Two

Note

For Abbie Hoffman

For Julius Hoffman

KU You

For K.

Rituals

That Moment

For Philip H. Schreyer, 1924-2005

Old Age

Suicide Note #1

Empathy

INTRODUCTION

In no way do I consider myself a poet. Nope. At best and most charitably, a stumbling *naif*. What I know about form, meter and structure is minimal. Mostly what I learned in college. My haikus are dodgy, my rhythms suspect. But I do write something *like* poetry every now and then and have since I was a kid.

It was a good way to interest girls. And get the bad stuff off my chest.

Stephen Sondheim wisely said that content dictates form, and sometimes something short and tight is what seems necessary to what I want to say at that particular moment—not something a novel or novella would explore, nor even something the length of a short story.

What's left but poetry?

So occasionally I give it a shot.

I've culled through years of these, dating back to the late 1960s, up through the present.

Trust me, you don't want to read the ones I've left behind.

I've been asked to publish them.

As with my men's mag stories in *Broken On The Wheel Of Sex*, I'm basically saying what the hell here. I'll risk it. Noose around the neck. Hoping for that reprieve from the governor. Which for my namesake never came.

Most of these are narrative pieces. Some even double as what Robert Swartwood calls Hint Fiction, wherein the lines break open to a wider imagined tale beyond. I'm a narrative writer and love stories and that sensibility leaks into the shortest of short-form too.

Though now and then it's sheer nonsense.

When I write this stuff, my goal, technically, is simply not to waste words, to cut as close to the bone as possible and still make some kind of sense. The other goal is to evoke something—thoughtful or tender or just plain silly.

And if that works for you even some of the time, I'm a-okay with that.

—Jack Ketchum, 4/26/13

JOHNNIE MACK BROWN

i'm sorry
to wake you
sheriff
but a man's
been
killed

HOBOE'S MEMOIR

Do you remember when we were both children,
that twilight summer spent in the Howards' abandoned home
behind the track?
The two of us, with splattered shoes and wrinkled denims,
the wife and husband of a thousand daydreams,
the proud parents of Joey and Jimmy and Linda and Steve—
all of them young,
as young as we wanted to be,
all of them trusting to us for blankets and supper
and a new pair of shoes come September.
And do you remember a night on the doorstep
when we hid in shadow from your father's voice calling us to
eat?
You and I, watching for first-star and youthfully spiteful—
we stood silent, barely touching, waiting for him to pass us by.
And I turned to you to laugh and tell you
that parents didn't hide on their own front porch—
it just was never done.
But you hushed me, pressed two fingers to my lips,
turned suddenly beautiful and broke my heart.

— For Chris Boyd, HOBOE

WHEN I AM A BOY

When I am a boy I stage a tournament
or settle into an Indian village
or find dinosaurs in the long grass.
When I am a boy I learn from books
or without them.
I sing myself to sleep.
I stay out after dark and rise early in the morning,
see myself in moonlight or sunlight,
run in the snow, swim.
When I am a boy I fight a forest fire
And doze in the shade.
When I am a boy I search for things.
Spiders on the windowsill,
a bird's nest,
hidden treasure,
the Big Dipper,
a tiny world beneath a rock.
When I am a boy I run along the grass
think hard and gather speed,
and I can fly if the wind is right,
right up through the trees.
I steal grapes from Mrs. Allen's yard
even though she'd give them to me if I asked
and they're sweet and they're juicy,
the best grapes in the world.
When I am a boy I sit on a rock
in the middle of a stream
picnic on Mrs. Allen's grapes
and I am never alone.

ARTHUR

He would never tell you this
but Arthur suspects
there is earth within him.
He swallowed a watermelon pit
and he is just a bit afraid
of what will grow there.

KU

Asleep I am
maiden and warrior.
Waking
I shall face riddles.

Jack Ketchum

KU TWO

I am always leaving
always staying.
No wonder
you distrust me.

11/11/87

Anyone sitting here?
The seat was empty.
Now, three years later that space is filled so completely
that not a mouse, nor a roach, nor a gnat
could squiggle in there.
We talked and the clouds and stewards' carts rolled by,
just talk,
just peanuts, vodka-tonic, scotch,
no jets outside the windows burning
and I remember turning to you,
feeling the weight of months lift away,
baggage handled finally,
so that in the end on a gamble,
as you were leaving,
I told you my name,
gave you my number,
you remembered them,
and now each night I see you there's aviation
and the steady thrum of wings
through every day between.

ANNOUNCEMENT

Ladies and gentlemen
due to atmospheric disturbances
we will resume the movie
after the following
atmospheric disturbances.
Yeeeeoooowwww!

BEAST

Beast always used to scare the shit out of me
leaping from the bed six feet up to the top of the hutch,
and those glass panes
a cat could crash through each time.
But I loved to watch her prepare and measure,
her eyes wide, haunches twitching, bracing,
getting it right.
And heart in throat I never once tried to stop her,
gasped, watched her hind feet slam the glass and
forepaws grasp the rim and lift her up
more gracefully than I'd imagined,
defeating the danger, getting it right.
She always scared the shit out of me every time,
cat and glass.
But it was what she wanted to do,
for all I know what she was meant to do,
and now that she doesn't,
age, cancer, frailty,
perhaps she's found some knowledge that
she simply shouldn't anymore
it's time she gave that up.

I never saw her fail.
I never saw her make the decision not to try.
I miss her courage and I respect her mind.
She settles with the same wide eyes for a touch.

CONTACT

What a cat does is complete you,
much as a lover will, much as a poem will.
The cat is not you but is of you
and in that sense only, she's yours.
That's quite enough.

Moments after she was dead
I cried the left lens out of my eye.
It rolled away down my cheek.
I felt like a goddamn fool, who needed to see.
I collected it
with her still lying warm across my lap
and tried to put it back again—
it seemed important.
But it wouldn't go,
wouldn't adhere.
I tried again,
it wouldn't go.
I was obsessed for a moment with the lens
with putting back the lens where it was supposed to be
so I could see.
It seemed important
so I tried again.
I put it in my mouth and rolled it across my tongue,
tasted salt and tried again and it wouldn't go,
wouldn't adhere.
But I wanted the touch and smell of her—
that was more urgent.
Especially the well-known scent of her,

the musk and perfume of her breath and fur,
so I crumbled the lens into a tissue and put it in my pocket,
said to hell with it
and did what I wanted to do and said goodbye.

The lens does not complete you.
The lens can not be urgent.
It's not necessary to see.
What a cat does is complete you.
In that sense, she's yours.

> For Beast
> 3/25/03

CATS HIDE NOTHING

Cats hide nothing.
You may have a hellova time,
should you care to,
trying to figure them out
but they're an open book.
Problem is, they wrote the fucker.

SLEEPING WOMAN

I watched you sleep.
Sleep is like a pause in life with nothing certain, no guarantees,
not even waking
just a passage from one breath to the next as neutral as the stars.
If there is a goddess of solace and renewal
she shows her face then,
perhaps only then,
when a loved one's face is free to age,
to sweep across planes from child to woman to crone,
when the flesh goes slack
and still awards such beauty,
such integrity
as to warn the heart
yet bind us,
devote us
forever to what we see.

FIREFLIES

I love you who bring me back in twilight,
hand in hand,
where we stand poised amid fireflies
and imagine cold heat in cold light.

HEARTS

Change of heart
Have a heart
Win my heart
Dear heart
The heart of the city
The heart of the problem
A card game in which
the object is either to avoid hearts completely
when taking tricks
or to capture all of them

FOR CAITY

Merry Christmas!
I give her to you, son
as balm, as solace, as responsibility, as love—
happiness in a puppy's eyes.
She's yours!
Look!
Pay attention and you won't be lonely.
She's my gift to you.

A child drifts, doesn't see,
misses the center.
The center was there Christmas morning.

So what of her then, this offering?
It's not in question.
The gift binds to the giver, the gift is wise,
sees her life's purpose,
knows love when she sees it
and responds in kind.
Between like souls there is no such thing as a gift,
only giving,
on and on.

CHRISTMAS DAY, 1969

Finally Christmas was all right
and I think it was because of the tree
which was all plastic needles
and coiled wire limbs with the
just the very tips painted different colors
so you knew where to stick them
and it was something on the whole
with band-aids dangling from white threads
and a bottle of downs potato chips chesspawns
a chew-stick and hash pipe all hanging from black loops and red
connecting tree to
watermelon rind cookie
decongestant toothbrush
fork and day-glo fangs
pantyhose clothespins nytol
and in the center
up top
to the left of one uglyduckling dangling limb misplaced
(electric blue tip notwithstanding)
a photo of me in beard and glasses
looking up and tired but up
telling somebody or other I wasn't having any.
My mother gasped and said *what*
and the rest was pure joy.

TO LANCE AND CATHY'S CHILD
ON THE AFTERNOON OF HER BIRTH,
JULY 9TH, 1970

It's a rinky-dink motherfucker of a world
you went and squirted yourself into, little girl.
It's got the blues and the shakes and the cops
and guns,
a bomb to scatter the whole trip
and no time to lose to let it be, let it be,
whispered words of five hundred thousand criminals
in a Georgia rockathonic spectacular
screwing and blowing dope and getting naked
like they were the only lovers left alive.
It's got Lester Maddox and Abbie Hoffman
pissing in the same tank,
it's got smack speed passion pornography
subversion perversion recession suppression
and something called One-A-Day to keep you fit.
It's got me and your old man
looking to Aeschylus and his Prometheus to show us
how to be a revolution
and now it's got you.

So what's up?
What the hell kind of language will you speak
to tell them you were born in nineteen-seventy?
Will you write them a letter or draw them a picture
or just think them straight through into yourself?
And what's in it for me?
How you gonna hold the hand

of a middle-aged flower child scribbler
when you are twenty-three and I am full of shit?

Suppose I tell you what I want from you.
And you can do as you damn well please.

First, you'd better be a badass little girl.
They'll have to respect the life in you
with none of this baby talk ninny-ninny-woo-woo
children-should-be-seen-and-not-heard crap
so you can speak right out
(if you expect to end your days understood then you'd better
begin there too.)
And when those two people who mingled you into this crib
see the size of your life and miss its scope,
(they will, no matter what they do)
forgive them but don't excuse them
and hold yourself yourself
in each of your changing seasons.

You can do us all a favor.
Live with love of what there is
just as you do today,
and when you want to touch the world of men
touch it with your whole body
and let men, touching you,
know all the power of the earth inside you,
of the sun and sky in your blossoming, blossomed breasts
(I can see it!
I can see it your wrinkled flesh,
in the whirl of your ears and in your toothless gums!)
Damn! I want you to jolt the world for a moment
with the simple power of all your nature held in joy
and damn! what a lovely day to sit beside you,
to speak with a soul who has no true parent but creation.

BILLY'S DAD

You never
done one wrong thing
but grow that mustache
but I'm telling you
that's what did it
to you
kid.

BETHEL, NEW YORK, AUGUST 16, 1969

It's a free concert
from now on
there's about 30,000 of you fuckers
out there I want you
to start singing.

A TERRIBLE THING

Someone's
done a terrible thing to me.
Someone
has made me incapable
of wanting to harm anyone.
Good grief.
That's a terrible thing
to do to a guy.

WINGS

Love has wings.
They open, accept,
close softly around the loved one,
clutch tight around the loved one,
hold true around the loved one.
But they're meant to open wide again too.
They're meant to soar.

MICHOU

So you're in the basement of a bar
and it's okay down there.
it's better than the street.
It's dark most of the time but you have good eyes
and you can see to avoid the bigger rats and stalk the mice.
You've been there as long as you can recall.
You're used to being alone
except when the double metal doors above the stairs
open and the street pours in.
Sounds that bleat throughout the night suddenly sharpen
into screams and wails that no animal has ever made
and footsteps hit the stairs and boxes hit the floor,
boxes pile up in front of you and all around
and maybe someone calls you by name
and you come out of hiding
long enough for him to scratch your head before he retreats
back the way he came.

You're a New York cat in the basement of a bar.
Now and then a woman who smells of foods
you've never imagined could exist
emerges down another stair
at the sound of a wooden door flung back
opens boxes and removes bottles
which bear the scent of earth and human sweat.
Michou! she says and puts down a plate of hard food
you could almost adore
were it not the same every day
and a bowl of water.

This woman is legion.
She changes so often
you can't keep sense of who she is.
Her skin is dark then fair then dark again
but she is kind.
She stops to scratch your head
and you make that sound again inside you
as you eat.
Sometimes she gives you a plate of food
some of it fine, some of it impossible to eat
before she retreats
back the way she came
amid the voices above
which sound to you like pleasure sounds,
then go muffled and later, silent.

You're in the basement of a bar.
It's dark down there but you can see.
Much smaller creatures than you
scuttle along the damp walls and floor
and you chase them or not according to your wont,
according to their trajectory
according to your interest.
Some have hard shells and are bitter.
Some have many long legs.
These are soft and tastier.
Some fly and make you leap.
Mostly you sleep.
It's cold.
It's hot.
You listen for the sounds.
Mostly you sleep.

You're a cat in the basement of a bar
and for a long time there's silence above,
no footfalls at all,
no footsteps on either set of stairs,

no hard crunchy food and no bowl of water,
no sounds of pleasure from above.
You lap the damp floor.
You listen.
Mostly you sleep.
It seems forever and you have killed the mice,
though few and very badly—
you're not much of a hunter.
But you've avoided the rats.
Your belly moans.

In the end you are nothing but sleep and dreams,
until the light streams down and you are lifted up,
suddenly awake in someone's arms
and moving up the stairs.

You lived in a basement, dark and damp.
A man lifted you up
and took you into the light.
The basement is nothing now.
You have lived forever in the light.

—For Neal and Victoria

AN HONEST WORD

An honest word
is one spoken to yourself
in the dark of night
with only you to listen
and only you to judge.

DREAMS THE LUNA MOTH

Dreams the luna moth—
Stars before him
ever sliding down
into night.

MONDO CANE

Sea turtle, from sand to sea—
Mother of Turtles, empty of seed,
senses her way, pushes her way back,
her burden passed upon the shore,
warm and growing under sand
she tossed to them for hours.
She was never made to turn the earth.
They await the form within them,
await the size to free themselves,
await the sun to dazzle the eyes and sear the flesh
and the rush to the sea to escape its sullen fury.
Overhead, wings and claws.
Below, awkward, shuffling toward the waves,
lives housed in new bodies.
Above, wings and gullets.
Beneath, sea spawn on the sand.

Mother of Turtles, empty of seed
knows nothing of the slaughter.
Decades ago she made her run,
was one of the few to survive.
Don't talk to me about endings.
Dare the beginnings.

ST. JOHN

The tide lifts the coral sand
and draws it out to sea.
An old woman across the way
sweeps her porch clean of fallen leaves.
A fish leaps from the water in the noonday sun.
And I,
who have been drinking wine since morning,
have a thousand days before me.
How can they fail
to move me from my chair?

GREECE

The press of hands together,
old, arthritic, mottled peasant hands,
this woman past all her years of strength and power,
hands pressed palms together
like a penitent.
The cold damp friction
as they revolve and clasp thumb to thumb,
then repeat,
the space between them trapped
lifeline to lifeline,
prayer and frisson, obeisance to stoicism,
moving slowly
to a glass of pale Athiri wine.

SWORD AND SANDAL

If I have to cross the Poison Sea
I'll find him.
I swear it
by the sacred bird of Odin.

CATS' HAIKU FOR PAULA ON THE ROAD

See us every day.
We know about adventure.
We'll await your eyes.

QUESTION

How will you greet me
that I will know you
in lands
we visit nightly?

SECOND VIRGIN

I don't know how she got under the chair.
The talk was pretty wild,
but exactly what preceded the event
I cannot say and will not guess.
(I was in another room.)
Only that her eyes were red-rimmed, filled with tears
that the muscles of her neck pulsed slow
and did not exactly match the rhythms
of her open mouth sucking
invisible teats
and breathing that it was a cage
she was in,
it was a cage with bars and all.

It took me a minute to pry her hands off the rungs
and another to talk her free,
lift her free of them,
and then a long while speaking of circuses and giraffes
candy apples and lemonade,
and the hottest summer of her life
when she was seven.
She stood up,
said in a weak voice that she had to go, and thanks,
and when I asked her *where*,
that she had to keep on moving and that was that.

Sometimes I see with such clarity.
I'm a man staring at the door to his cell,
understanding fully the walls around him.

REHEARSAL, MARAT/SADE, 1969

In the next cell a dead sparrow,
beak buried in flakes of poison
like white and yellow vomit.
Remember Hank Fischer, sir,
fuck the army,
scratched in deep above.

Metallic thunder
in the Fort Williams stockade,
deserted yet howling its past
in long straight shadows that cut across your brow.
The door slams shut
and you smell fear-sweat faint and unavoidable
(your own?)
hear impossible silences,
pace one two three four five
turn one two and
go a little mad here.
And I can't hold my arms out in front of me
for all the space we have here and I
lie on the rusted box-spring and count ninety-six stars—
no, ninety-eight stars etched above
which remind you where you are
and where you're not.

Marat/Sade is no simple play here,
Weiss no simple poet here.
Men passed their lives here.

So I lie back on the suspended springs
they called a bed
and there's Bill Galen's legacy signed beside me.
On bread and water—what a life.
Wednesday, April 4th, 1944.
Then Thursday Friday Saturday Sunday Monday Tuesday
over and over again
just below a length of chain,
so no one could see it but him.

POETIC

talked to Cynthia last night
she says she is quitting the theatre
they put her on call-backs
for an audition she did not go to

TV GUIDE

3:25
(2) Movie Western
"Law And Order"
A U.S. marshal encounters trouble
when he turns in his gun for a plow.
Ronald Reagan

MATHEMATICS

You still keep me awake until four,
but it's not us playing anymore.
I'm just awake, thinking numbers.
Four was our hour.
We'd look at the clock and groan.
We'd played the night through,
the sun almost rising but not yet.
Virtuous to sleep before sunrise,
to have loved the night away,
the hour of the wolf at hand,
but not yet,
not yet.
Four for us was always two plus two
plus two.

VINNI

Vinni's been a generous cat,
with me and with her sisters.
She failed today,
a buildup in her lungs,
she couldn't get her breath.
Now I'm not sure, at ten, whether she'll make it
till four in the morning,
the hour of the wolf they call it,
when those who are going to die, mostly do.

I watch the clock.
Each hour that passes is one she's still alive.
I've told both the cats she adopted, Zoey and Cujo,
to send her some cat-strength,
and Beastie too, who long ago adopted her,
and is dying of cancer—
I'd have thought she'd have gone before.

I've visualized her in all her favorite places, summoning her
calling her back to her apartment.
The box of books in the closet,
the high top shelf in the kitchen,
the window looking out onto the city street,
the couch, the bed, her place on the bed,
the place she sleeps with me on the bed,
the desk where she rests her head
against the carved wooden mahogany cat
beneath the warmth of a glass-and-pewter lamp,
as if visualizing will bring her back to her small apartment.

I'm performing magic here.

And then because she loved to dance with me,
big loopy waltzes when I was happy
or when I was sad,
I hugged the form of her in thin air
And smiled and cried
and danced us through the living room
and shook my fist to send her my strength too
and then sat down to write this as a prayer.

When I was sad she was the one I turned to.
I picked her up and danced.

The hour of the wolf eluded her.
She died around eleven.
I arrived in time to feel her breathing stop beneath my hand,
her heart stop beneath my hand,
Vinni asleep and looking straight into my eyes
as though I were really there.

And now the ghost of her is everywhere
in this small three-room apartment,
everywhere a cat can possibly get to—
box in the closet, shelf in the kitchen,
window and couch and bed, her place on the bed,
the place she sleeps with me on the bed,
the wooden cat beneath the cozy lamp,
and dancing through the living room,
sweeping across the living room,
big loopy waltzes, purring in my arms.

I can never—
I know I'll never—
dance quite that way again.

3/10/03

TRAGEDY

Tragedy's the fall from some high place.
Memory's the only way we're tragic.
All we've known, remembered,
gone.
That fall.
From that high place.

THE TEACHER, 1969

I will not wear your three-piece suit
but if you wish one for yourself
I know the name
of a fine and crafty tailor.

CRISIS

You have no time to be wrong—
the palace is in an uproar.
See
if you
can control
combustion.

FOR CUJO

We fail, we lose heart.
Cujo's failing.
It began years ago I think when Vinni died—
her first buddy, her surrogate mom
just disappeared one day.
She's never been quite the same,
never bonded to the other cats.
We were not enough to sustain her joy.
She'd known one better.

I brush her, make her clean and sweet-smelling and shine.
This she loves.
But she's old now and tired.
Food entices her or not
according to the day.
Mostly what's left is touch.
I brush her and she shines.
This she loves.
But I think she misses Vinni's touch
like a lost lover's
and my poor hands cannot suffice.

M.D.

The healing art is not my art.
I stand watch over the bad guys,
Those out there and those inside me,
report back and put them down as best I can.
That's all I do.
That's what I usually think.

But now there's this reach.
I feel this reach.
My arm feels stronger,
my fingers tighter,
more sure of the weapon.
(Surgical instruments can be weapons too.)

So I cut.
I cut deep inside me
and there you are.
Not a villain in sight.
I have to wonder
who's done this surgery?
Who's doctor to whom?

WALK

You just lumber along, old dog.
I'll follow.
What in hell you're smelling and enjoying so much
along this roadside
will always be beyond me
but here you are, having a fine time it seems
and if what they say is true, that in dogs the nose goes last,
this all seems pretty good to me.

So stop a while.
I've got time.
I'm ready to move when you are.

You fell again.
Those hindquarters giving way,
long before the rest of you,
long before heart and mind,
and don't forget that nose.
Well, that's what I'm here for,
to pick you up and get you started again.

You've seen the heron by the pond,
passed that same silly mutt
yapping down the street,
pissed this lawn and that
all along your territory,
as far as you can travel these days.
You're doing fine.

If only
you could let go of me.
I know you need to rest.
I know you hurt.
I know it's hard.
But because of me,
you won't let go.

It's me who's needing help right now.

There's such a thing as love at first sight.
And you, you're doing fine.

                       —for Caity, January, 2008

BETHEL, NEW YORK , AUGUST 16, 1969

everybody sit down
hold on tight to your neighbor, man
we're taxing the systems
the man next to you
is your brother
and you damn well better treat him that way
'cause if you don't
then we blow the whole thing
but we got it right here
hey everybody—
think real hard
and maybe we can stop the rain

JANIS

She's just screaming, she said.
But screaming is music.
All good music is screaming, variously controlled.
And its value is the measure of its cause.

A PROMISE

Almost ten years ago now
I promised a very good woman
not to fall in love again,
because my love could be toxic
to yet another woman
somewhere down the line.
It was almost bound to happen.
She knew whereof she spoke
and didn't wish me ill.
It was her honest appraisal.
I've kept that promise up to now,
Kept my distance.

I'm here because I'm selfish.
I'm here because there you were
and you stayed,
almost ten years since that promise.
I'm here because no se puede vivir sin amar.
Malcolm Lowry knew his shit too.
So I'm risking your neck
because I'm gambling
that this good woman was wrong back then,
that you and I have much to do.

What's toxic maybe
is not to believe in love.

MORNING STAR

I lived for you awhile,
You were my morning star,
The reason I woke.

IMPERATIVES

Write the word "duel."
Change the "l" to a "t."
Write again.
Write the word "evil."
Spell it backwards.
Choose.
Watch two people kissing.
Realize that it's a conspiracy.

ON "THE GATES," NYC

It's heraldry!
Passing beneath the fabric
we become knights and ladies,
a chivalric moment in Central Park.
The pace slows—
an impromptu parade,
trace-memories of a pace centuries old,
yet new to us, and transitory.
In sunlight the color is saffron,
delicate warm flavor of the east.
In shade,
the west, the energy of molten steel.
They waft and twist and mingle.
Both colors please the eye,
Fire and warmth in February.
Where but here in this long garden
will we find the east, the west
and a quiet parade
of gentle knights and ladies?

CATSKILL MORNING OBSERVATION

We heard church bells in the morning.
Charles said, my mother always claimed
that if you hear church bells in the morning
you must be in love.
Amusing but ridiculous I thought.
Was everyone in town in love?
Does carrying a torch count? I asked him.
Yes, he said.
I said, okay.

THE LETTER

So there it is on paper,
a hint at least why she's lost to you.
She doesn't paint you as a villain.
You've done nothing wrong, she says.
But you've done everything wrong.
If you'd been bigger, more understanding, less rigid,
if you'd been there as a lover
when a lover was necessary.
But she doesn't paint you that way.
She's generous,
you're off the hook.
But you have your own hook.
She can dare things you can't,
which is the way it should be
when you're young.
But you're not young.
You may never see this again,
feel this again,
and you can almost accept that,
But you can't, not quite.
You want to bite the reaper's hand,
bite into the soft strong flesh of her
which stays that hand.

CLOCKING

It's going to be many years, love,
before you wonder if you'll last till morning,
wonder when all you've done and not done
will catch up with you.

When you fall in love in your fourth quarter
you know that chances are
it's not supposed to happen,
that love's for the first and second quarter
or maybe even the third
but the fourth's already proven itself
something of a bitch.

Then you meet someone
who doesn't seem to get it,
doesn't seem to know about quarters and clocks
winding down,
not your clock anyway,
She's blind to it.
That would be you, love.
And you think, maybe you can
blow the whole damn world of time away.
Maybe it can always last till morning.

IMPERATIVES TWO

keep
your
sunny
side
up
wrap
your
troubles
in a
dream
let
a smile
be
your umbrella
and
go cat go

NOTE

Dear whomever is using this dryer.
A pair of my pants
is now freeloading with your wash.
I got caught in the rain
And my pants got wet
And I really need them.
So please don't hate me
or be disgusted
or throw them away
or steal them or anything,
okay?
Emergency rules?

FOR ABBIE HOFFMAN

All I know is
on a cold winter night
you can't snuggle up
to a voting machine.
If you folks will excuse me
I've got some fudge in my briefcase.
It's easier to get now (what isn't?)
But war has a way
of making little moments
seem big at the time.

FOR JULIUS HOFFMAN

Like you told Bobby Seale,
if you speak once again
while the jury is in the box
and I have to send them out again,
we will take such steps
as are indicated by the circumstances.

KU YOU

Who are you
but an orchard
where men lie restful?

FOR K.

I will always miss
who I was
when we were.

RITUALS

We had our rituals.
You'd climb up on the microwave mornings.
I'd reheat the coffee
Sixty seconds
And scratch your belly.
You'd squint and knead the air
Until we heard the beep.
I'd run the dishwasher
And clear the counter above,
Rising heat for basking cat
Until the dishes were done.
I'd pick you up
And you'd mark me,
Cheeks and chin,
With each side of your mouth.
Claiming me.

THAT MOMENT

The old cat blinked once,
focused,
then was lost to her forever.

FOR PHILIP H. SCHREYER, 1924-2005

On my uncle's death
I thought of how my life was slowly emptying out
of all the people who made it rich.
It was inevitable,
all the big souls disappearing.

In the mirror tying my tie for his service
I made a Windsor knot,
one of the few I'd had to bother with these days
since nine to five wasn't an issue anymore,
not for a long time,
but I made the knot,
my fingers remembering the loop and pull instinctively,
the knot a part of me by now,
and realized looking into the mirror
that when I was just a kid
it was my uncle
who had taught me how to make that knot
because mine was sloppy
and the girls were going to notice.

He'd saved me that indignity.
He's sold me on the knot,
the beauty of the knot.
He'd seen the man within the boy,
knew the man was going to need it,
and knew as a salesman that you could sell anything
if you believed in it enough,
to teenage girls or grown-up men

if it was firm and true.

My uncle was a man's man
but a soft man,
who was still a boy,
who remembered the boy inside the man
In himself or in me,
and thought that
you never really needed to grow up exactly
so long as you shouldered your responsibilities,
tied the knot when you needed to,
did your best, laughed at your fears,
knowing there was nothing funny at all
about your fears,
but that laughter could beat it nearly every time
if the salesman in you believed it,
and if it was firm and true.

He was a man's man but a soft man,
unafraid to love wife or dog or sons or daughter,
or to reveal love.

So he taught me how to tie the knot,
that Windsor,
wise and elegant.
He sold me a bill of goods.

The big souls don't disappear.
What they do is live inside the knot.
A knot is a binding together of loose ends
into something strong and true.

OLD AGE

Time is entropic,
love, anti-entropic.
I have the balance of the universe inside me.
Every cell and circumstance which time pulls apart
my interests draw together.

SUICIDE NOTE #1

Nanny, didn't we all say
"In God we trust?"
Didn't we, Nanny?
And didn't He take the store?

EMPATHY

Here's this cat.
He's fallen asleep
in your hand.
He knows
you will never
use that hand
against him.

7/26/13

About the Author

Jack Ketchum's first novel, *Off Season*, prompted the *Village Voice* to publicly scold its publisher in print for publishing violent pornography. He personally disagrees but is perfectly happy to let you decide for yourself. His short story "The Box" won a 1994 Bram Stoker Award from the HWA, his story "Gone" won again in 2000—and in 2003 he won Stokers for both Best Collection for *Peaceable Kingdom* and Best Long Fiction for *Closing Time*. He has written twelve novels, arguably thirteen, five of which have been filmed: *The Girl Next Door, Red, The Lost, Offspring*, and *The Woman*, written with Lucky McKee. His stories are collected in *The Exit at Toledo Blade Boulevard, Peaceable Kingdom, Closing Time and Other Stories*, and *Sleep Disorder*, with Edward Lee. His horror-western novella *The Crossings* was cited by Stephen King in his speech at the 2003 National Book Awards. He was elected Grand Master for the 2011 World Horror Convention.

Curious about other Crossroad Press books?
Stop by our site:
http://store.crossroadpress.com
We offer quality writing
in digital, audio, and print formats.

Enter the code FIRSTBOOK
to get 20% off your first order from our store!
Stop by today!

www.ingramcontent.com/pod-product-compliance
Lightning Source LLC
Chambersburg PA
CBHW030800150426
42813CB00068B/3307/J